FREE THROW SHOOTING

Psychological & Physiological Techniques

By Coach Bob Reinhart

Decatur High School
Decatur, Georgia

CHICAGO REVIEW PRESS
820 N. Franklin, Chicago, IL 60610

First edition
Second printing
ISBN 0-914091-11-5

Book and cover design by Siemens Communications Graphics.
Published by Chicago Review Press
820 N. Franklin, Chicago, IL 60610

Table of Contents

Photographs

About the Author

Coach Reinhart is a native Hoosier from Dale, Indiana and played basketball at Indiana University under the late Branch McCracken.

He has been Varsity Basketball Coach at Decatur High School since 1970 and his teams have participated in the Georgia High School State Play-offs for 10 of the last 12 years. Under Coach Reinhart's guidance, Decatur has won two State AAA Championships and has been runner-up on two occasions and his overall record at Decatur is 285 wins and 67 losses for a winning percentage of 81%.

Coach Reinhart has been named Region Coach of the Year and State of Georgia Coach of the Year on several occasions. He has also won Coach of the Year honors from the Dekalb Tipoff Club and the Atlanta Tipoff Club. He has written several articles for various basketball publications and he is a sought-after speaker for basketball clinics.

Acknowledgements

I would like to express my sincere appreciation to my good friend, Randy Pennington, for his guidance and suggestions in the preparation of this manual. Also, my thanks to Louise Plankenhorn for her assistance in editing.

I would also like to offer my gratitude to my son, Bobby, who assisted with the shooting fundamentals and demonstrated the correct and incorrect physiological techniques of free throw shooting.

Bob Reinhart

CREDITS

Photography: Eddie Fowlkes

Photographs: Bobby Reinhart

There is More to it than Thinking and Practicing

After many years of coaching, I have heard a million times that free throw shooting is "repetition, repetition, repetition." Or else, free throw shooting is "all between the ears." And I must admit that for years, without reservation, I adopted, adhered to, and taught these philosophies.

After much in-depth mental analysis and after several frustrating experiences of using anything I could think of and anything I could read, I have come to the conclusion that there are some important free throw techniques or fundamentals, including both PSYCHOLOGICAL and PHYSIOLOGICAL, that a lot of players are not aware of and consequently do not practice.

The ideas I am sharing in this manual are tested and will, if practiced and enforced properly, lead to better GAME-SITUATION free throw percentages. Too many times a player is permitted to "slide by" with improper shooting habits, mentally and physically, only to be frustrated when his team loses a close game because of poor free throw shooting. Looking back on my coaching career, I can vividly recall some of our players who shot free throws incorrectly, and I did not make the effort nor take the time to teach them correctly. And, yes, several times we paid for it. You see, I bought these "repetition" and "thinking" theories without really noticing or questioning whether the techniques were correct.

I am thoroughly convinced that it does absolutely no good to shoot a hundred or even a thousand free throws, and that repetition is not worth a nickle unless the psychological and physiological techniques are correctly and properly instilled in every player.

The "all between the ears" theory had also been a thorn for several years. "You can hit 'em if you think you can" used to be a favorite with me. But the real truth is that a lot of players "think" they are good free throw shooters and still cannot hit 50%.

An INWARD, sincere confidence is the result of experiencing FREQUENT success; thus, a player cannot be honestly confident by hitting 50%, because that is certainly not an indication of successful shooting. Probably the primary reason for his lack of success, IF HE IS BEING HONEST when he says he has confidence, is an incorrect or uncorrected physiological shooting technique. If a player is permitted to continue to use improper shooting methods, then obviously his GAME-SITUATION free throw percentage will not improve. And it may get worse, i.e., if "imperfect practice makes imperfect." Then what results is a lack of confidence and total frustration. The old adage that "practice makes perfect" is very misleading. Only "PERFECT PRACTICE MAKES PERFECT", and in free throw shooting, as well as in playing golf, the psychological and physiological techniques are both important.

Be Careful with Comfortable Positions

"GET COMFORTABLE" was another of my favorite expressions. And there is nothing wrong with this instruction except that there are too many "degrees of comfort" among players. A player may feel comfortable with his feet eight inches apart but that position is not a good free throw shooting position (Photo #1). He may feel comfortable with his elbow too far outside the body (Photo #2) or his feet pointing to the sideline, but these positions are not good physiologically. He may feel comfortable shooting from the end of the free throw line (Photo #3), but according to simple mathematics and body alignment, this position is incorrect for successful shooting.

If we observe closely we will notice that some players assume stances or positions that are comfortable, ACCORDING TO THEM, but which are really fundamentally unsound from a physiological standpoint. Consequently, they need to be corrected immediately. In a lot of instances, a player will assume a certain stance or position because he wants to imitate another player even though the stance may not be comfortable for him. So sometimes we have to "show" what a comfortable free throw position looks like, BASED ON TESTED TECHNIQUES AND PERCENTAGES.

INCORRECT

1

2

INCORRECT

3

A few years ago I thought a player should be given the freedom to select a "comfortable" position and then practice, practice, practice. But I can assure you that this technique will not work and will not improve GAME-SITUATION free throw percentages if the "comfortable" position is physiologically incorrect!

I realize some players may vary their positions slightly, but the fact remains that there are still tested physiological techniques that are better suited for successfully shooting free throws. Obviously, if a player already has a shooting method or routine and can consistently hit 80%-85% of his GAME-SITUATION free throws, he should be left alone, regardless of his techniques. However, this seldom happens because good free throw shooters use the proper techniques ON EVERY ATTEMPT.

Only Confidence Causes Relaxation

Another expression that I frequently adhered to before I stopped to analyze what I was saying was "RELAX!" This was thought to be meaningful and encouraging to a player, especially if he missed two or three free throws in succession. And, after all, I had heard other coaches use it for years, so I thought this was good advice, only to realize that it is impossible to relax physically, at least totally, unless one is relaxed mentally. SINCE MENTAL RELAXATION COMES FROM CONFIDENCE AND CONFIDENCE COMES FROM FREQUENT SUCCESS, the admonition to "relax" after a missed free throw is meaningless, as far as being helpful.

Instructing a player on the correct techniques will result in building confidence which leads to mental relaxation and in turn culminates in physical relaxation. This may seem elementary; however, I can assure you that you can tell a player to "relax" on every free thow and his GAME-SITUATION free throw percentage will not improve until the relaxation is brought on by confidence and success at the line. You cannot cause relaxation by simply saying the word. If players KNOW they have good free throw shooting fundamentals and techniques, they will be relaxed on every attempt.

Developing the Proper Perspective

We would not even think of beginning the basketball season with old, worn out, weather-ridden basketballs, but yet many players and some coaches practice day after day and year after year with either little or no effort to correct improper free throw shooting techniques. We seem to fall into a trap, continuing to accept mediocre free throw percentages, and then feel content on the night our team shoots 65%-70% from the line.

For years I just accepted that some players would be good free throw shooters and other players would be poor free throw shooters. That is, until I came to the realization that ALL close games can be decided by something as simple as a FREE throw and that ANY DEDICATED PLAYER WITH PRIDE can be a good free throw shooter! With this realization firmly planted in my mind, it was at this point I determined that ALL OF MY PLAYERS WOULD BE INDOCTRINATED REPEATEDLY ON THE CORRECT PSYCHOLOGICAL AND PHY-SIOLOGICAL TECHNIQUES OF FREE THROW SHOOTING. There is a possibility, although an infrequent one, that a player may not have the ability to perform at the line as well as other players, but nonethe-less he can still improve by using the techniques in this manual.

I CONTINUE TO BE AMAZED AT THE LACK OF EMPHASIS, THE CAREFREE AND NONCHALANT ATTITUDE, AND THE LACKADAISICAL APPROACH THAT A LOT OF PLAYERS HAVE TOWARD FREE THROW SHOOTING. Just take a few seconds and dwell on the word FREE. All players and coaches need to realize that we do not get many uncontested FREE throws. Players must be constantly reminded and made aware that most of the time they must be prepared to shoot on the move, or at least against some kind of defense.

So one of the initial psychological techniques needed to improve GAME-SITUATION free throw percentages is to critically analyze, and then to completely eliminate the general connotation of the word FREE. In too many cases, when something is FREE and we know it, we have a tendency to play it down as being unimportant and we do not take it very seriously. This is the time where a good "psychology" lesson comes in handy, and this is where a few minutes out of practice sessions to constantly remind the players that a FREE throw is not really FREE at all is time well spent. Players must be made to realize that someone did something to earn, or at least cause, the foul to be committed. Players should be constantly reminded that absolutely nothing in this game is FREE except their admission to the game . . . and they have to make the team to get that!

Instructions which Lead
to Incorrect
Concentration Techniques

Granted, one of the key psychological techniques in GAME-SITUATION free throw shooting is proper CONCENTRATION. However, the OBJECT OF CONCENTRATION is more important! I have heard many philosophies and have read many books on free throw shooting, and practically all of them tell players, in essence, "not to look at the scoreboard before attempting a free throw because the score is unimportant." Or else, the "first free throw is just as important as the last one." I just cannot comprehend this type of instruction being beneficial! I will assure you that all players WILL look at the scoreboard regardless of instructions not to do so and also regardless of the score. To me, telling a player not to look at the scoreboard is like telling someone not to think of an elephant . . . after telling him, it will be impossible for him to think of anything else. This type of instruction, in my opinion, will not work.

We do not want the OBJECT OF CONCENTRATION to be the scoreboard, but at the same time we do not want to tell our players something that will be impossible for them to do. If emphasis is placed on not looking at the scoreboard in our practice sessions, then in an actual game situation a player will automatically think he has "done something wrong" when he glances at the board . . . although he really CANNOT keep from doing it. Consequently, this negative thought will be an incorrect psychological technique and just might prevent him from TOTAL and CORRECT concentration.

Obviously, the first free throw in a game is important, but all of us who have been involved in games either as a player or a coach know that SOME SITUATIONS ARE INFINITELY MORE CRITICAL THAN OTHERS. Statistics do show that if a team hits its first three or four free throws, the team as a whole will probably have a good shooting night at the line . . . which again points out the importance of the mental aspect. However, to say that a free throw at the beginning of the game with the score 4-1 is just as important as a free throw with the score tied and two seconds to play does not make a lot of sense to me. We do not want to underemphasize the importance of ANY free throw, but we do want our players to understand that there are GAME-WINNING SITUATIONS where free throws are involved, and it is at these times we expect DEDICATED PLAYERS WITH PRIDE TO HAVE TOTAL AND UNDIVIDED CONCENTRATION!

The Correct Object of Concentration

Before attempting free throws, we do not want our players having needless conversation with anyone . . . teammates, opponents, fans, officials . . . not ANYONE. However, we do use a phrase of encouragement on EVERY free throw, "MAKE HIM PAY FOR IT!" We have found this admonition to be very simple and very helpful.

Obviously, timeouts might dictate conversation on some occasions although we generally do not call a timeout when we are shooting, i.e., under normal circumstances. There are, I think, good psychological reasons for a shooter not involving himself in needless conversation at this time. A free throw shooter's concentration should be on one thing and one thing only . . . MAKING THE FREE THROW. A free throw situation is one of the very few parts of the game when a player can TOTALLY concentrate about one thing and not have to be concerned about anything else. It is during a free throw situation that INDIVIDUAL PRIDE can be determined.

This TOTAL concentration on the COR-RECT OBJECT can be easily mastered if the player IS A WINNER.

In explanation, the player who committed the foul either made a good play or he made a mistake. If the free throw is made, the offender made a mistake, generally. If the free throw is missed, the offender made a good play, generally. Now, either the free throw shooter is going to go away from the line a winner, if he makes it, or a loser, if he misses. With this SOLE THOUGHT in mind, a free throw shooter has the opportunity to be a WINNER on every shot. Consequently, the OBJECT OF CONCENTRATION FOR THE FREE THROW SHOOTER IS THE MAN WHO COMMITTED THE FOUL, and we now have a game of competitiveness on EVERY free throw.

All WINNERS thrive on competition and relish this type of "personal confrontation." Players who use free throws as a personal challenge will be GOOD free throw shooters in most situations and GREAT free throw shooters in critical situations.

Perfect Practice Makes Perfect

All teams spend hour after hour of practice time on all kinds of offensive manuevers, defensive sets and alignments, ball control, rebounding and fast break fundamentals, special situations, etc., and of course all of these are integral parts of the game. It is the intention of all coaches to leave no stone unturned as far as game preparation is concerned. Then does it not make good sense to practice CORRECT free throw shooting techniques, both psychological and physiological, EVERY DAY? I am not talking about shooting 100 or 200 free throws at the end of practice sessions, but rather the INTENSIVE practicing of PER-FECT techniques and fundamentals. IT IS THE QUALITY OF MENTAL AND PHYSICAL EXECUTION AND NOT THE NUMBER OF FREE THROWS PRACTICED WHICH LEADS TO BETTER GAME-SITUATION FREE THROW PERCENTAGES!

If we are to practice ALL free throw shooting fundamentals, we must begin with the designation of the shooter and include such things as the psychological techniques of "taking a foul" properly, heading to the free throw shooting circle, toeing the line for the shot, correct body alignment and finally, the proper and correct physiological techniques.

The importance of executing these techniques properly and the importance of using psychological and physiological fundamentals the SAME WAY, EVERY TIME, EVERY DAY cannot be overemphasized! It takes a lot of time and a lot of practice to do these techniques CORRECTLY . . . BUT IT TAKES THE SAME AMOUNT OF TIME TO DO THEM INCORRECTLY! Correct execution will result in better free throw percentages EVERY DAY. And you will see your team winning those CLOSE GAMES AT THE LINE, making all the time and effort worthwhile.

Taking the Foul
and Heading to the Circle

When a free throw shooting situation occurs, the designated shooter should move swiftly to the top of the free throw shooting circle but should not TOE THE LINE at this time. I do not mean that he should sprint or even run but by not walking slowly, he is assuring himself that he is eager to shoot the free throw. One word of caution here . . . anytime one of our designated free throw shooters has been knocked to the floor, we do not want him getting up quickly. We want him to get up very non-chalantly, casually letting everyone know, including the officials, that a foul definitely occurred. After he has "recovered", he then proceeds to the top of the circle. This method of "taking a foul" has a definite psy-chological ploy to it in that sometimes a player who gets fouled will get up too quickly and the official may think sub-consciously that a foul may not have been committed. By getting up "slowly", we assure the official that "the right call was made." If a player is going to use psy-chological techniques in game situations, these same situations must be simulated over and over in the practice sessions.

We want our players who will be filling the lane slots on the free throw to walk slowly to their positions, thus giving our shooter complete assurance that we have confidence in his ability to hit the shot(s) and that we are not even thinking of rebounding. Obviously, we ARE ready if the shot is misfired.

We want no conversation at this point except the comment "MAKE HIM PAY FOR IT" by teammates on the floor. We want no conversation directed to our shooter from substitutes, managers, etc. TOTAL concentration is the key at this point. We want our shooter to concentrate his thoughts solely ON THE MAN WHO COMMITTED THE FOUL, and now we have a game of ONE ON ONE. Now is where "the rubber meets the road" because either the shooter or the offender is going to emerge a WINNER in this confrontation.

It takes extraordinary concentration after a player takes a "hard foul" not to show any signs of anger or frustration, at least momentarily. However, the player who disciplines himself and the one who knows and believes that TOTAL CONCENTRATION is the difference between success and failure at the line, will simply get off the floor, head to the top of the circle, and get ready to MAKE SOMEBODY PAY FOR IT!

In our game-type scrimmages, we will call a time out occasionally after a foul to let our players get accustomed to this situation. In other words, WE DO NOT WANT ANY GAME SITUATION TO OCCUR THAT WE HAVE NOT EXPERIENCED AND PRACTICED BEFOREHAND. The only thing that might be different is crowd noise. However, if a player has been conditioned to concentrate on THE RIGHT OBJECT, if he has INDIVIDUAL PRIDE, and if he is CONFIDENT of his psychological and physiological techniques, nothing will bother him at this point.

We will also have some of our players in our game-type scrimmages to try to distract our free throw shooter by talking to him and harassing him as we know some of our opponents will. Here, again, we are simply placing emphasis on situations that when we experience them in a game, we will be totally familiar with them and we will be able to adjust to them more naturally.

Toeing the Line

When all players are in their lane positions and the official is ready to hand the ball to our shooter, we want him to move to the line, BUT NOT BEFORE. We do not want our shooter waiting to shoot either before the officials are ready or before the other players are in their positions or before possible substitutions are made. We want our shooter to TOE THE LINE WITH THE BALL. When toeing the line, the position we prefer is one foot slightly in front of the other, STRONG FOOT FORWARD, with an obvious space between the lead foot and the line (Photo #4).

There should NEVER BE A TIME when a free throw shooter is called for a line violation, and there will not be if the shooter maintains a state of TOTAL concentration. If a player lines up too close to the line, then his concentration may be on the placement of his feet rather than the business at hand.

If at any time after our free throw shooter has been handed the ball by the official and the official blows the whistle for any reason, or if the horn is sounded which sometimes occurs, we want our shooter to hand the ball back to the official, if he will take it, and START THE ROUTINE COMPLETELY OVER

(Photo #5). Many free throws are missed because of broken concentration, and any delay at the free throw line after a shooter's routine has been started will most certainly affect the shooter.

4

5

Body Alignment

The correct alignment of the body on the free throw line is one of the most important physiological techniques in shooting free throws, just as correct body alignment is an important fundamental in golf, i.e., for hitting the ball in the right direction. We want our players to line up with the STRONG foot, right foot for right handers and left foot for left handers, slightly ahead of the other POINTED DIRECTLY TO THE CENTER OF THE RIM (Photo #6). In this alignment, the shooting hand and arm will automatically be lined up with the target, the center of the rim, at the release of the ball (Photo #7). BY USING THIS TECHNIQUE ALONE, A PLAYER WILL BE AMAZED AT HIS IM-PROVEMENT AT THE LINE! One cannot overemphasize the importance of having the feet SQUARED UP (Photo #8).

In a lot of instances a player will consistently miss free throws by hitting the right or the left side of the rim. In carefully checking body alignment and foot placement, we frequently find the player's STRONG foot out of position and aimed directly toward the right or left side of the rim instead of directly toward the center of the rim (Photos #9 and #10).

We NEVER permit our players to stand on either side of the free throw line. We simply explain to them that we will allow them to align themselves differently whenever the rules committee decides to change the location of the rim on the backboard.

CORRECT

6

7

CORRECT

8

INCORRECT

9

INCORRECT

10

Developing a Routine

We insist that all of our players have a set routine before attempting a free throw. We do allow freedom in some areas as to what a player wants to use, but we have some techniques that work better than others so we expect our players to use them. We are very specific with our players as to which techniques are optional and which of them are mandatory. A lot of our individual routines are optional as long as they are within the psychological and physiological framework of tested techniques. IN ALL INSTANCES, HOWEVER, WE INSIST THAT THE SAME ROUTINE BE USED ON EVERY FREE THROW!

After our shooter toes the line and receives the ball from the official, we want him TO GRIP THE BALL WITH THE SEAMS (Photo #11). A correct grip is a fundamental necessity in shooting a basketball properly. As a matter of fact, it may be said to be the first physiological fundamental because it will be impossible to release the ball CORRECTLY if the ball is not gripped CORRECTLY. The "with the seams" grip serves a dual purpose . . . it allows for better control of the ball and it becomes a vital part of the overall shooting routine. It is something a player will ALWAYS remember to do when he receives the ball from the official and it is the BEGINNING of his routine. The shooting hand should be in the center of the ball, slightly to the right, for right handers, the opposite for left handers (Photo #12). The balance hand should be placed on the left side of the ball with the thumb just below the center of the ball. To teach this CORRECT shooting position, we use the SURE SHOT SHOOTING AID which can be purchased from most basketball suppliers.

CORRECT   CORRECT

11   **12**

The shooting hand should be cupped, which will not allow the "heel" of the hand to touch the ball. It is impossible to get the correct "backspin" on the ball if the shooting hand is too far to the right side of the ball or too far to the left side of the ball (Photo #13). Both of these positions will result in "sidespin." With this type of rotation on the ball, only a "perfect" shot will go in the basket. A ball with "sidespin" that hits any part of the rim will have very little chance of hitting the glass and banking back into the basket (Photo #14).

After assuming the proper grip, a player should proceed with his individual routine. The routine may include bouncing the ball three or four times or whatever. The number of bounces is strictly an individual matter but the important thing is that the SAME NUMBER OF BOUNCES BE USED ON EVERY SHOT. If, in practice, a player is noticed taking two bounces before the first attempt and four bounces before the second attempt, he should be corrected immediately because a different routine before each attempt will result in formulating an incorrect routine, which is exactly what we are trying to cure.

Some players like to extend the arms upward and backward behind the head and make three or four jerking motions with the ball. This, too, is a good routine but THE NUMBER OF JERKING MOTIONS SHOULD ALWAYS BE THE SAME. Some players like to place reverse spin on the ball and bounce it out in front of them two or three feet so that it returns to them. Here, again, this routine is fine AS LONG AS IT IS ALWAYS THE SAME. And some players like to use a combination of several routines.

THE PLAYER WHO DOES NOT PRACTICE A DEFINITE ROUTINE FOR EVERY FREE THROW WILL NOT BE A GOOD PERCENTAGE GAME - SITUATION FREE THROW SHOOTER. A good routine, based on an individual's preference within the framework of TESTED techniques, will build confidence and will develop a sense of pride every time a player steps to the line. This is extremely important in CRITICAL situations when a player must be in COMPLETE CONTROL.

After our shooter has completed his routine, we want him to "eye the basket", take a deep breath, and place the ball "chest high" directly in front of the body, just before releasing the ball (Photo #15).

INCORRECT

13

14

CORRECT

15

Releasing the Ball

Most of our instructions have been related to the psychological and physiological techniques which prepare a player for the best possible concentration, exclusive of the actual shooting of the ball. The process of the releasing of the ball includes the use of the legs, sighting the target, correct elbow position, finger-tip control and follow through.

We teach the physiological techniques of free throw shooting using the A, B, C method before the actual release. That is, Aim, Bend, Cock. When aiming, the sight target should be "the whole goal." We do not like to teach the sighting of the front of the rim or the back of the rim as our target BECAUSE THAT IS NOT WHAT WE ARE TRYING TO HIT! After sighting and before the shot, the legs should be bent comfortably. LEG POWER IS ESSENTIAL IN PROPER FREE THROW SHOOTING. Before releasing the ball we want our players to have their knees bent slightly and then bend them more just prior to pushing off (Photo #16). At the same time a player cocks the ball for the shot, he should be bending his knees. FOR PERFECT TIMING AND RHYTHM, THESE SHOULD BE DONE SIMULTANEOUSLY. If the knee bend is slow, then cocking the ball must be done slowly; if the knee bend is quick, then the ball must be cocked quickly.

In the actual release the ball should roll out over the tips of the four fingers giving the ball a natural backspin. This backspin will act as a "brake" whenever the ball hits the rim or the board and will permit more of the "off-center" shots to drop in. As the shooter thrusts the ball forward, he should push up with the balls of the feet, straighten the legs and push the ball FORWARD AND UP to gain the necessary arch on the ball. To attain this arch, the arm and hand should reach up above the target as the ball is released (Photo #17). The center release point should be between the index finger and the middle finger. When the shooter pushes the ball forward and up, the wrist will flex forward automatically.

When released, the ball should slide out of the balance hand. The balance hand after the ball is released should be in the same position it was in before the ball was released (Photo #18). THE BALANCE HAND SHOULD NEVER BE THRUST FORWARD WITH THE SHOOTING HAND! (Photo #19).

After releasing the ball, the follow through should result in the shooting fingers pointing toward the center of the rim and the THUMB POINTING DIRECTLY TO THE FLOOR (Photo #20).

CORRECT

16

CORRECT

17

CORRECT

18

INCORRECT

19

CORRECT

20

Correct Psychological Free Throw Shooting Techniques

1. CORRECT techniques breed CONFIDENCE.

2. Relaxation will be a RESULT OF FREQUENT SUCCESS.

3. The general connotation of the word FREE must be eliminated.

4. Glancing at the scoreboard is a NORMAL act and SHOULD NOT BE DISCOURAGED.

5. Free throw attempts should be made ONLY when a player is in COMPLETE CONTROL OF HIS EMOTIONS.

6. There should be no NEEDLESS conversation by the shooter or by his teammates. The saying "MAKE HIM PAY FOR IT" is ample admonition.

7. EVERY free throw has a WINNER and a LOSER.

8. The correct OBJECT OF CONCENTRATION is essential.

9. A PSYCHOLOGICAL routine is just as important as a PHYSIOLOGICAL routine.

10. INDIVIDUAL PRIDE is at stake on every
    GAME-SITUATION free throw.

Correct Physiological Free Throw Shooting Techniques

1. A PHYSIOLOGICAL routine should be developed on EVERY attempt.

2. Grip the ball correctly . . . WITH THE SEAMS.

3. Point the STRONG FOOT toward the CENTER OF THE RIM.

4. Keep the elbows in . . . POINTING ALMOST TO THE FLOOR.

5. Keep the head still . . . NO SNAPPING.

6. ALWAYS toe the line WITH THE BALL.

7. A . . . Aim: SIGHT THE WHOLE GOAL.

8. B . . . Bend: GIVES YOU LEG POWER.

9. C . . . Cock: SIMULTANEOUSLY WITH THE BENDING OF THE KNEES.

10. Develop the CORRECT RELEASE:

   A. Roll the ball OFF THE FINGERS FOR CORRECT BACKSPIN.

   B. Reach FORWARD AND UP on the release.

C. Keep the balance hand IN THE
ORIGINAL POSITION.

D. Follow through . . . POINT THE
FINGERS TOWARD THE RIM AND THE
THUMB TOWARD THE FLOOR.

Practicing Free Throw Shooting

1. BEFORE ACTUAL PRACTICE BEGINS
   FOR THE DAY
   A. General shooting should ALWAYS
   be done ON THE MOVE, with absolute-
   ly NO SHOOTING AND WALKING
   AFTER IT.

   B. Free throw shooting should be practiced ALONG WITH GENERAL
   SHOOTING.

   C. Players should shoot 8-10 jump
   shots from different distances and
   positions on the floor and then should
   step to the line for 2 FREE THROWS,
   USING INDIVIDUAL ROUTINES.

   D. Players should continue alternating
   jump shots and free throws but should
   not shoot MORE THAN 2 FREE
   THROWS AT A TIME while shooting
   around.

2. DURING SCRIMMAGE SESSIONS

   A. Always shoot ONE PLUS ONE
   FOULS and TWO SHOT FOULS.

   B. Keep ACCURATE records and
   statistics on scrimmage free throw
   shooting and KEEP THE PLAYERS

INFORMED as to their individual progress.

C. ALL PLAYERS SHOULD USE INDIVIDUAL ROUTINES ON EVERY FREE THROW IN SCRIMMAGE SESSIONS.

3. AFTER SCRIMMAGE IS COMPLETED AND BEFORE PRACTICE ENDS FOR THE DAY

A. Free throws should be practiced EVERY DAY AT THE END OF PRAC- TICE. Using the correct techniques, this procedure can make a poor prac- tice end up GOOD and a good practice end up GREAT.

B. Players should shoot 2 free throws and move until EACH PLAYER HAS ATTEMPTED 50 FREE THROWS. With four goals and four players to a goal, this takes about 15-20 minutes. THERE SHOULD BE ABSOLUTELY NO TALKING AT THIS TIME AND PLAYERS SHOULD BE IN LANE POSITIONS.

C. Emphasis at this time should be on PRACTICING AND DEVELOPING INDIVIDUAL ROUTINES. All players should be CAREFULLY OBSERVED FOR CORRECT TECHNIQUES AT THIS TIME.

OR

A. Each player will go to the line for a two shot foul. If he misses the first one, HE RUNS TWO SPRINTS. If he hits the first one but misses the second, HE RUNS ONE SPRINT.

OR

A. Each player will go to the line for a two shot foul. If he misses the first attempt, EVERYONE AT HIS GOAL EXCEPT THE SHOOTER, RUNS TWO SPRINTS. If he hits the first but misses the second, EVERYONE AT HIS GOAL, EXCEPT THE SHOOTER, runs one sprint. You will notice, using this procedure, that some QUICK PRESSURE will soon be placed ON THE SHOOTER by those at his goal!

A GOOD TECHNIQUE TO USE AT THE END OF ALL PRACTICE SESSIONS IS TO DISMISS PLAYERS INDIVIDUALLY AFTER THEY MAKE TEN FREE THROWS IN SUCCESSION. This, too, will develop into a PRESSURE situation especially from an INDIVIDUAL PRIDE standpoint.

**Three Important Pre-Tournament
Free Throw Shooting Hints**

1. DON'T CHANGE A THING!

2. DON'T CHANGE A THING!

3. DON'T CHANGE A THING!

NOW IS THE TIME WHEN ALL OF THE PSYCHOLOGICAL AND PHYSIOLOGICAL TECHNIQUES WHICH HAVE BEEN COR-RECTLY TAUGHT AND PRACTICED WILL PAY OFF FOR YOU AND "MAKE YOUR OPPONENT PAY FOR IT!"

Techniques, Ideas and Instructions That Will NOT Improve Critical Game-Situation Free Throw Percentages

1. Telling players that ALL free throws are EQUALLY important.

2. Telling players that "placing the index finger on the air-hole" serves as a good CONCENTRATION OBJECT.

3. Shooting 100 consecutive free throws every day BEFORE practice.

4. Shooting 100 consecutive free throws every day AFTER practice.

5. Shooting 100 consecutive free throws ANYTIME.

6. Telling players they must "THINK" they are good free throw shooters. (USELESS WITHOUT THE CORRECT TECH-NIQUES.)

7. Telling a player to "GET COMFORT-ABLE."

8. Telling a player to "RELAX"!

9. Telling a player "NOT TO LOOK AT THE SCOREBOARD."

10. Telling a player to TALK TO "SOME-ONE" before shooting a free throw in order to relax.

11. Telling a player to grip the ball "ANY-WAY THAT FEELS GOOD."

12. Telling a player to toe the line "ANY-WHERE THAT FEELS RIGHT."

13. REWARDING players for making free throws and PUNISHING them for missing.

14. AND ON AND ON AND ON . . . . .

ALL OF THE ABOVE TECHNIQUES AND IDEAS SOUND GOOD AND, BELIEVE ME, I HAVE TRIED THEM ALL! BUT THE FACT REMAINS THAT GAME-SITUATION FREE THROW PERCENTAGES WILL NOT IM-PROVE UNTIL A PLAYER DEVELOPS AND USES THE CORRECT PSYCHOLOGICAL AND PHYSIOLOGICAL TECHNIQUES AND DEVELOPS AN INDIVIDUAL ROUTINE IN WHICH HE HAS COMPLETE CONFIDENCE!

I sincerely hope that all players and coaches who read and study this manual will make a concerted effort to follow the tech-niques, ideas, instructions and principles included. If so, I will assure you that GAME-

SITUATION free throw percentages will improve greatly.

Throughout this entire manual, I have illustrated tested techniques that will improve GAME-SITUATION free throw percentages. I am not at all interested in determining which players can hit 50 consecutive free throws in a practice setting. What I want to know is which player I can depend on to develop a correct psychological and physiological routine and the player I can depend on to hit those critical free throws "WHEN THE FANS START CHEERIN' AND THE POPCORN STARTS POPPIN'!"

I make no claim that the psychological and physiological techniques and fundamentals in this manual are all-exhaustive. However, they are the best I have found and if practiced correctly, a 60% shooter will become a 70%-85% shooter. More importantly, players will make more of those CRITICAL GAME-SITUATION free throws and many of those close games will end up in the "W" column.